Water Adventures

Will Tripp

sundance™

A Haights Cross Communications ® Company

sundance
A Haights Cross Communications ✦® Company

Published by
Sundance Publishing
P.O. Box 740
One Beeman Road
Northborough, MA 01532–0740
800-343-8204
www.sundancepub.com

Water Adventures
ISBN 0-7608-9636-4

Illustrations by Kevin Rechin; pp. 15, 23, 27 (bottom) Jim Kopp

Photo Credits
Cover ©Stephen Frink/CORBIS; p. 1 U.S. Navy photo by Photographer's Mate Airman Ryan O'Connor; p. 6 (center) Central Press/Getty Images, (bottom) David Watt; p. 7 (top) ©Bettmann/CORBIS, (center) Graham Beech; p. 8 courtesy of Ken Warby; p. 9 (top) Keystone/Getty Images, (bottom) courtesy of Ken Warby; p. 10 (top) Quicksilver (WSR) Ltd., (bottom) American Challenge, Inc.; p. 11 Quicksilver (WSR) Ltd.; p. 14 (top) ©Teru Kuwayama/CORBIS, (center) U.S. Navy photo by Photographer's Mate Airman Rob Gaston, (bottom) ©Bettmann/CORBIS; p. 15 U.S. Navy photo by Photographer's Mate Airman Rex Nelson; p. 16 (top) U.S. Navy photo by Airman Joe Hendricks, (bottom) U.S. Navy photo; p. 17 (top left) U.S. Navy photo by Photographer's Mate Airman Apprentice Eric Cutright, (top right) U.S. Navy photo by Photographer's Mate 2nd Class Aaron Ansarov, (full page) U.S. Navy photo by Photographer's Mate 1st Class Richard J. Brunson; p. 18 U.S. Navy photo by Photographer's Mate Airman Tommy Gilligan; p. 19 (top left) U.S. Navy photo by Photographer's Mate Airman Kristopher Wilson, (bottom left) U.S. Navy photo by Photographer's Mate Airman Ryan O'Connor, (right, from top to bottom) U.S. Navy photo by Photographer's Mate Airman Justin R. Blake, U.S. Navy photo by Photographer's Mate 2nd Class Daniel J. McLain, U.S. Navy photo by Photographer's Mate Airman Ryan O'Connor, U.S. Navy photo, U.S. Navy photo by Photographer's Mate 2nd Class Michael Watkins; p. 22 Rod Catanach ©Woods Hole Oceanographic Institution; p. 23 Tom Kleindinst ©Woods Hole Oceanographic Institution; p. 24 ©Woods Hole Oceanographic Institution; p. 25 (left) ©Ralph White/CORBIS, (right) ©Stephen Frink/CORBIS; p. 26 (left) Brian J. Skerry/National Geographic Image Collection, (bottom) photo courtesy of NOAA/UNCW; p. 28–29 courtesy of Joachim Hauser, Hydropolis Underwater Resort Hotel; p. 29 ©Carl & Ann Purcell/CORBIS
Printed in Canada

Table of Contents

Full Speed Ahead!

Look! Up in the air! It's a bird! It's a plane! It's a . . . boat?

When traveling at low speeds, a **hydrofoil** is just a mild-mannered boat floating through the water. But when it speeds up, something remarkable happens: it begins to fly! Equipped with a set of underwater wings called **foils**, the boat rises high into the air, leaving only the foils in the water. Without all that water to slow it down, the hydrofoil can move at speeds that few boats can match.

But the fastest boat in the world is the **hydroplane**. Instead of floating above the water, hydroplanes skim across it at incredibly fast speeds. How fast do they go? Who has the fastest boat? You'll have to keep reading to find out. Bon voyage!

The Dangers of Speed

Cruising through the water at hundreds of miles per hour is very exciting. It is also highly dangerous, and people have even lost their lives on fast boats.

Life in the Fast Lane

The Englishman Donald Campbell lived for speed. In the 1950s and 1960s, no one was faster than Campbell, both on land and on water. In 1964, one of his cars reached a speed of 403.1 miles per hour, a world record! But Campbell was even more famous for his records on the water. In 1955, his jet-powered hydroplane, the *Bluebird K7*, broke the world's water-speed record, traveling at a speed of 202.32 miles per hour. He would go on to break his own record six more times!

Campbell is the only person to hold the world water-speed record and land-speed record at the same time.

Campbell racing his famous Bluebird K7

Donald Campbell

Parts of Campbell's boat were finally recovered in 2001.

Tragedy on the Water

Even with all of his success, Campbell was still determined to go faster. On January 4, 1967, Campbell was attempting to become the first man to go over 300 miles per hour in a boat. On the first of two required runs, Donald's boat reached a speed of 297 mph. Campbell quickly tried again. This time his boat reached 300 mph, but then it flew into the air, turned upside down, and crashed into the water. Hitting the water at that speed is like hitting a thick wall of concrete. Pieces of **debris** from the boat flew everywhere, and Campbell was killed.

Donald Campbell's World Water-Speed Records

Date	Boat	Speed (mph)	Location
July 23, 1955	*Bluebird K7*	202.32	England
November 16, 1955	*Bluebird K7*	216.20	United States
September 19, 1956	*Bluebird K7*	225.63	England
November 7, 1957	*Bluebird K7*	239.07	England
November 10, 1958	*Bluebird K7*	248.62	England
May 14, 1959	*Bluebird K7*	260.35	England
December 31, 1964	*Bluebird K7*	276.33	Australia

Broken Record

The world's fastest boat—was it built by scientists?
Was it driven by a professional racer? The answers
may surprise you . . .

The Need for Speed

Ken Warby is just a regular guy
from Australia. He's also nicknamed
The Fastest Man on Water. Why?
Because Warby built and raced the
world's fastest boat: the *Spirit of
Australia*. While Warby was building
the 27-foot hydroplane under a tree
in his backyard, he had one goal in
mind: to break the world water-
speed record.

When Warby broke the record, his
engines were not even at full power!

He first broke the record on November 20, 1977, at the Blowering Dam in Australia. Traveling at a speed of 288.60 miles per hour, Warby just barely broke the previous record of 285.21 miles per hour. Most people would have been satisfied with this achievement, but not Warby. Just one year later, Warby tried again. This time he not only broke the record—he shattered it. Warby's speed record of 317.60 miles per hour has stood for over 25 years!

Ken Warby poses in 1978.

THE SPIRIT OF AUSTRALIA

The *Spirit of Australia* has a missile-like shape designed to make it travel as fast as possible.

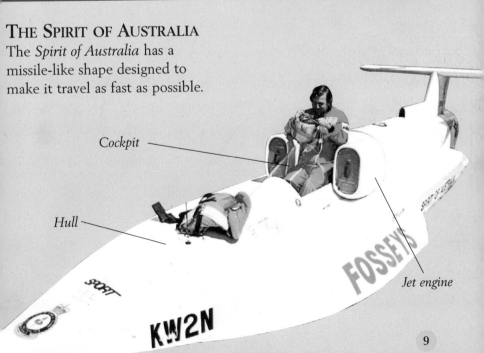

Cockpit

Hull

Jet engine

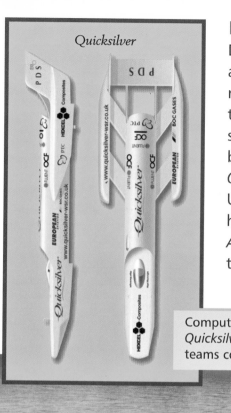

Quicksilver

Playing Catch-Up

Despite all the danger, people are still trying to break Warby's record. In Great Britain, a team of engineers and other specialists are building a brand-new boat called *Quicksilver*. A team from the United States is building its own hydroplane as well. The boat, *American Challenge*, is designed to go over 400 miles per hour.

Computer images like these help the *Quicksilver* and *American Challenge* teams construct their boats.

American Challenge

The *Quicksilver* team plans to race their hydroplane, which has a Rolls Royce engine.

In 1980, a racer named Lee Taylor came close to breaking Warby's record. He built a boat made to travel at a speed of 600 miles per hour! During his attempt to break the record, however, disaster struck. Taylor died when the *Discovery II* spun out of control and sank beneath the water.

Everyone still trying to break Warby's record is facing stiff competition . . . from Warby himself! Now in his sixties, Warby is building a brand-new boat in an attempt to break his own 317.60 mile-per-hour record.

How Do I Break the Record?

So you think your boat can break Ken Warby's record? Not so fast. To officially break the record, your boat must complete two 0.62-mile long straightaways. If your boat reaches an average speed greater than 317.60 miles per hour, then congratulations! You now hold the world water speed record. Just make sure someone appointed by the Union of International Motorboating is watching or your record won't count.

City at Sea

Welcome to the aircraft carrier
***U.S.S. Enterprise* CVN 65!**
Established: 1960
Population: 5,500
Location: Somewhere on the ocean

Over the years, ships just keep getting bigger and bigger. Who would have thought they would get this big? The *U.S.S. Enterprise* and the many aircraft carriers like it are among the biggest ships in the world. These massive boats can transport up to 85 fighter jets all over the ocean.

The United States uses aircraft carriers to respond to problems anywhere in the world. Because over 5,000 people are needed to run them properly, aircraft carriers are almost like cities floating on water. So hop aboard and get ready to learn all about these "floating cities." Hope you don't get seasick!

Carrier City

It may be called a city on the sea, but an aircraft carrier is not your typical city.

Get Lost!

Aircraft carriers do not have streets or roads like cities do. What they do have, though, is passageways—miles and miles of them! With all of those winding passageways, it can be easy to lose your way. To make things less confusing, many of the thousands of **compartments**, or rooms, of an aircraft carrier have maps to help crew members find their way through the maze.

Aircraft carriers have over 900 miles of pipes, cables, and wires that carry water, air, and electricity throughout the ship.

The *U.S.S. Enterprise* is 1,101 feet long. That is taller than most skyscrapers!

The Chrysler Building

Cross-Section of an Aircraft Carrier

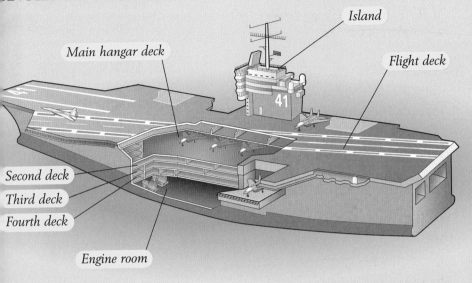

Island

Main hangar deck

Flight deck

Second deck

Third deck

Fourth deck

Engine room

It's a Living

Just like in a city, people onboard an aircraft carrier have their own specific jobs. Some work in the **hangar** and tend to the planes. Others make sure the carrier sails smoothly through the water. You will also find many jobs on a carrier that people do on land. Each carrier has several doctors, dentists, and barbers. And, of course, there are many jobs related to feeding thousands of people.

Just Like Home

So what do people on an aircraft carrier do when they are not hard at work? Well, they could grab a bite to eat at one of the **mess halls** that can serve up to 18,000 meals a day. With enough food on the ship to feed 6,000 people for 60–90 days, hunger is not a problem! And if the crew gets bored, they can always watch one of over 3,000 televisions onboard. They can even listen to the radio. Aircraft carriers have their very own radio stations that broadcast right from the ship!

Crew members can call home to their loved ones from one of over 2,500 phones onboard.

How Are Aircraft Carriers Built?

First each section of the ship, from the flight deck to the hangar, is built separately. Then thousands of people work together for years to assemble the ship. They use powerful cranes that can lift sections weighing 900 tons! Even when the carrier is complete, it must go through several months of tests and trials before it can be sent out to sea.

Some crew members may stay below deck for weeks without seeing the ocean or the sky.

The flight deck is a dangerous place, so it is off-limits for many crew members.

Ready for Takeoff

Flying planes off an aircraft carrier and then landing them again is no easy task. It takes over 2,000 crew members and some unique equipment to get the job done.

Up, Up, and Away!

On land, planes always have plenty of room to get off the ground. But planes on an aircraft carrier don't have this advantage. If a plane takes too long to fly into the air, it will go straight into the ocean! Aircraft carriers have a clever way around this problem—steam **catapults** that act like giant slingshots. Once a plane is placed in the catapult, a sudden rush of steam pushes it into the air. The steam is so powerful that the planes can reach their top speed of 165 miles per hour in only two seconds. That's twice as fast as most cars!

Wrong way, guys!

The color of a crew member's shirt tells what job that person does. A person with a yellow jacket helps direct the planes.

Plane taking off

Landlocked

Landing a plane on an aircraft carrier is dangerous. Each jet has a hook attached to its tail. When a plane is ready to land, the pilot aims to try and hook onto one of four thick wires that are placed across the deck. After a plane catches one of the wires, it is quickly pulled in for a safe landing. If a pilot misses the wires on the first try, he must turn around and make another pass. You know what they say, "If at first you don't succeed, fly, fly again!"

Plane landing

F-18 Hornet

F-14 Tomcat

E2C Hawkeye

5-3B Viking

EA-6B Prowler

Delving the Depths

Some call outer space the "final frontier." But what about the ocean? There is an entire world beneath the waves just waiting to be explored.

Mysterious creatures, colorful **coral**, islands on top of undersea mountains—all these things and more can be found in the ocean. Small submarines known as submersibles are exploring this mysterious underwater world even as you read this. With the help of these undersea crafts, scientists have made many maps of the ocean and discovered several new forms of life. They have even uncovered sunken treasure from shipwrecks!

But there are still many mysteries within the ocean just waiting to be unlocked. With over two-thirds of Earth covered in water, scientists have barely scratched the surface of this unknown world. Who knows what they will find next?

Super Submersible

When it comes to exploring the ocean depths, *Alvin* is the best. But *Alvin* is not a person. It's a submersible!

A typical *Alvin* dive lasts for 6–10 hours.

A Deep Diver

In 1964, *Alvin* was first launched into the ocean. Since then, the craft has made over 3,600 dives all over the world! *Alvin* may be small (it can hold only three people), but it is very strong. Its **titanium** shell protects those inside from the powerful water pressure and freezing temperatures of the ocean. Thanks to *Alvin*, scientists have plunged as deep as 4,500 meters (14,700 ft) into the ocean. That's almost three miles straight down!

ALVIN STATISTICS

Height	
	12 feet
Weight	
	35,200 pounds
Cruising Speed	
	3,000 feet per hour
Max Speed	
	12,000 feet per hour
Life Support	
	3 people for 72 hours each

These are some of the instruments used to operate *Alvin*.

Alvin can do more than just dive, though. Its bright searchlights can light up the darkest parts of the ocean, up to 40 feet in each direction! *Alvin* also has several video cameras so scientists can record their explorations. *Alvin* even comes with two robotic arms and a small cage used to collect rocks, sand, and undersea creatures. Equipped with so many useful tools, *Alvin* has helped scientists make some amazing discoveries.

INSIDE THE *ALVIN*

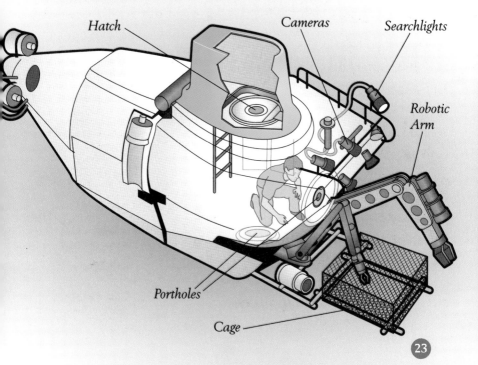

Hatch

Cameras

Searchlights

Robotic Arm

Portholes

Cage

Tubeworms have no mouths. Instead of eating bacteria as most creatures do, they absorb it into their bodies like a sponge.

No Sun? No Problem!

Plants and animals need sunlight to survive — or so we thought. In 1977, a group of scientists used *Alvin* to make a routine dive near the Galapagos Islands. At a depth of 8,000 feet, where no sunlight could possibly reach, *Alvin* flashed its light upon an astonishing discovery. There was life everywhere! Blind crabs, dragon-like fish, tube-like worms...how could all these strange and mysterious creatures exist without sunlight? Thanks to *Alvin*, that question was soon answered.

Turn it off, I'm getting dressed down here!

The scientists on board *Alvin* noticed that the creatures were all huddled near a **hydrothermal vent**—an underwater geyser that constantly erupts hot water. The water was so hot that it melted *Alvin*'s thermometer! Some substances in these powerful bursts of water provide **bacteria** with energy. And many sea creatures feed on the bacteria.

The water from hydrothermal vents can reach temperatures of up to 750°F!

BOBBING UNDER THE SEA

Check out this new way to explore under the water! This vehicle is called a breathing observation bubble—BOB for short. Air is pumped into the large plastic bubble that covers the rider from head to shoulder. The tank, located on the front of the BOB, holds 40 minutes worth of air.

The bottom-heavy BOB easily stays upright in the water. The seated rider presses buttons to change direction. Riders are supervised from above and below, so bobbing along in a BOB is quite safe.

Home Is Where the Ocean Is

It would be much easier to explore the ocean if we could live down there. Thanks to modern technology, now we can do just that!

Aquarius underwater

Home Under The Sea

Imagine looking outside your window and seeing colorful corals and tropical fish in your backyard. Picture going for a swim simply by stepping out your front door. This is what life is like at the *Aquarius* research station. Located about 65 feet below the surface off the coast of Florida, it is a unique underwater laboratory. On the outside, the *Aquarius* looks like an underwater spaceship. Once you get indoors, though, it is more like a house. There is a shower, a toilet, a refrigerator, a microwave — all powered by its very own diesel generators. With all the comforts of home, why would you ever leave?

When it is not is use, *Aquarius* can be lifted back onto land.

Undersea Studying

A lot of serious work goes on in the *Aquarius*. The scientists onboard are constantly studying the undersea world around them. With so many things to study, a team of scientists typically spends up to 10 days at a time living in the research station.

Living in the *Aquarius* is quite safe. But when scientists go back to the surface, they have to be very careful. When someone spends a long time underwater, a gas called nitrogen builds up in the body. If he rises too quickly, the nitrogen will make him sick. It could even kill him! A person must travel up through the water very slowly so that the nitrogen has time to leave the body. So it can take someone several hours to reach the surface again!

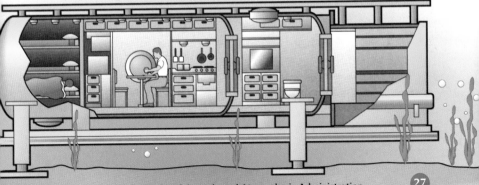

These scientists are relaxing inside the Aquarius.

NOTE: Aquarius is owned by the National Oceanic and Atmospheric Administration (NOAA) and operated by the University of North Carolina at Wilmington.

What's Next?

At least one architect has a plan for the world's first underwater luxury hotel. His name is Joachim Hauser, and his plan is to build the Hydropolis Hotel in the waters of the Persian Gulf off the city of Dubai in the United Arab Emirates.

His hotel design includes three linked elements: a wave-shaped aboveground land station, a jellyfish-shaped underwater hotel, and a submerged transparent train tunnel.

There go the guests' dinners

This illustration shows an above-water view of the futuristic Hydropolis Hotel.

JULES' UNDERSEA LODGE

Up to six guests can stay at Jules' Undersea Lodge. But they have to scuba dive to enter it because it is located 30 feet deep in Emerald Lagoon in Key Largo, Florida. The lodge is equipped with hot showers, a modern kitchen, and videos for entertainment. Guests can relax and view the colorful, undersea wildlife through the windows.

The plan also includes two **translucent** domes that break the water's surface. One of those, covering the hotel ballroom, will even have a **retractable** roof. And if this hotel becomes a reality, it will cost you only about $5,000 a night to stay there!

Other people are even thinking about the possibilities of underwater villages. Will that ever happen?

Only time will tell!

Fact File

Feet Below Sea Level

0–450 ft

Sunlight Zone
Most marine life—
fish and plants—live in
this zone.

450–3,300 ft

Twilight Zone
Some sea creatures have
built-in light organs that
make them glow. But it
is too dark and cold for
plants to grow.

3,300–13,000 ft

Dark Zone
Fewer creatures can
survive here where food
is so scarce.

Swordfish

Sea turtle

Dolphin

Jellyfish

Tuna

Shark

Angler fish

Viper fish

Squid

Snipe eel

Tubeworms

Submersible

White crab

Glossary

bacteria tiny organisms some underwater creatures use for energy

catapults devices for launching an airplane at flying speed

compartments rooms of an aircraft carrier

coral colorful, organic material found in many oceans

debris the remains, or pieces, of something that is broken apart

foils underwater wings that raise some boats out of the water

hangar the section of an aircraft carrier where planes are stored

hydrofoil a boat that rises out of the water at fast speeds

hydroplane a fast boat that skims across the water

hydrothermal vent an underwater geyser

mess halls dining rooms on board an aircraft carrier

retractable able to be pulled back

titanium a very strong metal used to build many types of crafts

translucent clear enough to let light pass through

mess hall

Index